GW00722625

THE CIRCLE OF LIFE

THE CIRCLE OF LIFE

REPLACING HARDSHIP WITH LOVE

WALTER MIKAC

MACMILLAN
Pan Macmillan Australia

First published 1999 in Macmillan by Pan Macmillan Australia Pty Limited
St Martins Tower, 31 Market Street, Sydney

National Library of Australia Cataloguing-in-Publication data:
Mikac, Walter.
The circle of life.

ISBN 0 7329 0975 9.

1. Mass murder – Tasmania – Port Arthur. 2. Bereavement – Psychological
aspects. 3. Grief. I. Title.

157.937

Typeset in Goudy by Midland Typesetters
Printed in Australia by McPherson's Printing Group

PREFACE

E ach and every one of us will be confronted by a major challenge in our lives. When we have to face adversity or hardship we can choose to shut down, retreat into our safety zone and not participate in life, or we can decide to learn from the experience and make a difference to the lives of those around us. Dealing with the bittersweet symphony of life creates a path of self-discovery and transition for all of us.

We sometimes find it hard to express our feelings and yet they play such an important role in our enjoyment of life. A positive attitude is the key. There will always be others in a worse situation than our own, and we should not lose sight of that. Being true to my emotions has led to much soul searching but the self-awareness that has resulted from it is worth every bit of effort.

This book is a collection of observations, reflections, feelings and positive affirmations that have helped me deal with tragedy and still be able to view the future with optimism. I believe there are thoughts in this book that will help each and every one of us.

What is most evident to me is that the power of love is the energy of the universe. It sustains us when we most need it and provides us with the enthusiasm to reestablish who we are. I have had a fortunate life. There has been an abundance of love from my family and friends. There has been nurturing, care and compassion. There has been love and devotion for Nanette and my beautiful daughters, Alannah and Madeline. There is now love and commitment for Kim. Love has inspired in me a new zest for life and the belief that, with her, no situation is unconquerable. It is my wish that others may gain hope from this. I have discovered who I am and my sense of purpose. Kim, I am eternally grateful.

In the end, no matter what our fears, anxieties or trepidations are, we need to have hope for the future. A vision whereby the world does have empathy and love. An enriching cradle for our children to grow up in. Live. Enjoy. Appreciate each and every day and make the most of what you have.

Dedicated to the power of love

Some people expect your level of mourning to be a monument to your loved ones. This expectation really makes it hard to be yourself. It makes you lose your ability to act spontaneously and with enthusiasm. Tell people that you're still allowed to be yourself. I try not to get too concerned about what other people think.

Empathy is not necessarily riding the rollercoaster but knowing what the nausea feels like when you've finished the ride.

I find it essential now to tackle emotions and conflict as soon as they arise. This has a twofold benefit. Firstly, it allows you to know exactly where you stand in a situation and then how to deal with it. Secondly, it means that those thoughts are not cluttering your thinking any more and wasting valuable time.

Turn every stumbling block in your life into a stepping stone for the future.

Families are such important influences in our lives. They should be there to brace and support you in the difficult times but should not be overbearing or stifling. At some point in our life we must discover our identity and grow independently. If your family nurtures this, well and good; if not, there is no time like now to spread your wings and fly.

Grief is such an individual thing that the only sure aspect of it is that it takes *time*. Do not be in a hurry to get it over and done with. It is gradual and I suppose it is a natural reaction to try and not bring the hurt back. Each revisit will hopefully be a little easier and eventually the past will sit harmoniously with the future.

Birthdays, anniversaries and Christmas will inevitably bring memories of lost ones flooding back. Try to ride the wave of emotions as it comes and know that within a day the worst will be over.

❧

I forgive all in my past
Thus I am free to move into the future
I have supreme hope for what is ahead
I will embrace it with enthusiasm and glee
The opportunity is there for me to create.

I am thankful for what I have and have had
It has been given to me by God
I will use all my ability and potential
I must achieve all that I am capable of.

When beginning a relationship, think not of the love you will receive but of what you have most to give. Listen, learn and be patient. Perseverance is of the essence.

❧

For your body and soul to merge with that of another, there must be integrity. Honesty with regard to our failures and successes, our strengths and weaknesses. Finally we need to be honest about our expectations and ambitions, for we make our own destiny.

Look at yourself in the mirror each morning and admire what you see. Reaffirm in your mind the uniqueness and brilliance that is you. Each and every one of us has something special that sets us apart from others. Take time to acknowledge and appreciate your individuality. There is only one you.

The light of day is for everyone to see. It's only when you've stopped to experience the mystery of life and what's all around you that the light can be so brilliant and guiding. A few seconds each day is your gift of appreciation. Close your eyes and stand on some grass, fill your lungs with air, put your arms in the air and feel the energy of the universe. In the prospect of spending another marvellous day on the planet open your eyes to a new vista.

❧

As thoughts are the first stage in our behaviour, it makes sense to make them positive.

❧

Often people have said to me, 'I don't know that I would have been able to continue in your situation.' Why? What have I found within me that has given me the nurturing to survive? One of my fiercest battles has been with patience. After facing major adversity in our lives, be it a life-threatening illness, the ending of a relationship, the loss of a job or career path, or whatever unforeseen or tragic circumstances are thrust upon us, we must take time to reflect and regroup. Gathering thoughts, dreams and all our emotions in a cohesive way. Being positive so that the lessons learned from the past can lay the foundations for the future. Probably from the time I finished my pharmacy degree I knew that I would be successful. Without initial guidance this took a little longer than anticipated to achieve. What I did have, though, was an innate belief in my own ability. Some people grapple with this all their lives. I know that I can achieve anything I set my mind to. And so, your mind and attitude are the only limiting factors in life.

❧

For the observer trying to help someone deal with grief, here are some of the things that may be useful:

- Listen, listen, listen and do not draw judgement.
- Never say you know how the other person feels (even if you have been through the exact situation your reaction would be different).
- Be positive and try not to put negative conotations on the deceased person simply because they are gone.
- Let the grieving person do whatever they feel like doing to get them through another piece of time.
- Give hugs and kisses in plentiful supply.
- Share your good memories of the deceased person.

Treat those you love like the reflection you see in the mirror. Want them to achieve their full potential, to be secure and content in everyday life and to have dreams that are endless.

~

W ords do not transpose to actions, so let your actions do your speaking.

❧

A child's instinct is to emulate the parents that brought it into the world. Hence, as a parent and educator, our example can never be underestimated.

The role of a parent is that of a gardener. You prepare the environment and plot for your planting. With the essentials for life in abundance we plant the seeds and wait for germination. One of the mysteries of nature is that we never know how long this will take. The plant sprouts forth with vigour and form. With care and attention it thrives on the energy of the universe. We watch its structure develop and increase in complexity. There comes a time when the strain of new growth needs support. Thus as a parent we need to provide the stake. To give our creation the anchor from which to blossom. With the stake it will gain its backbone and skeleton for the future. The odd trimming may be required to help build shape and form but the stake will remain. As in life's garden, the gardener's work is never complete. Even once the plants are mature they continue to need water and fertiliser to flourish in much the same way as every child needs praise and reassurance. Food for the soul and balance for the excesses of life. Garden with passion and love but do not stifle your garden by not letting go.

The power of love and creation will always triumph over the power of destruction and revenge.

Men have the amazing ability to believe they have verbalised thoughts that have churned around in their heads. I find it useful to say it out aloud when it springs to mind. When comfortable, allow your emotions to let the words flow. Speak from the heart and the results will amaze you.

❧

I see the world with great clarity
I will resolve problems as soon as they arrive
My world will be calm, peaceful and serene
I am in harmony with the universe.

I start the day with vitality and energy
I am healthy and proud of it
Enthusiasm runs through my veins
I want to make a difference
I feel strong and decisive
I am a winner.

❧

Regrets are the refuse of the soul. They are only useful to learn from as the lost opportunities of our lives. They should not serve to torment us but to drive our enthusiasm for life and others. If we are patient, it is possible the chance will occur again.

❧

To regret is to be beholden to the past. To hope is to hold on to the future.

There are difficult and painful experiences from throughout my life that I would rather not have endured. Each and every one of those experiences has, however, developed me as a person. It has allowed me to see life from a lateral perspective, a view from which there comes exultation. This allows tragedy and sadness to sit alongside exhilaration and contentment. As if they were scales, there must be balance in our lives, for without it we don't allow ourselves all the world has to offer.

Nourish the soul with life's virtues. Set aside time to reflect and to let growth occur. Quiet time serves to reassure us. It is imperative that to care and love others we treat ourselves in this way first.

The rewards of rejuvenating yourself are manifold. The stronger your cup overflows with love, the more that is available to shower on those around us.

To love someone is to know them as well or better than they know themselves. The aim is to see life through their eyes. Touch the wonders around us with their touch. Smell the fragrance in life and breathe its air as they do. Consciously put yourself in the shoes of your partner so that despite how good they might look on the outside, you can feel where the leather is rubbing on the inside as well.

Be aware of your mortality. Despite feeling invincible, life is transient and mystical. Losing sight of this clouds our vision of today.

Success in life cannot be measured by material wealth and achievement as it is no longer ours when we leave. The money in our bank accounts does not stay there but is disbursed. What does measure our success is the deposits of joy we have left in the hearts of those left behind.

❧

Break the shackles of life and be inspired. Leave behind the despondency of the economy and the despair of work. To be complete we must be in touch with our own spirit and that of a greater power. Strive to know yourself better and everything around you will be clearer.

What we call mistakes are in fact the most potent road to learning. Everyone needs the latitude to make a decision and then to deal with its consequences. The nature of what we discover depends on whether we see life holistically. Often the self-development afforded by a major 'mistake' is proportional to how we suffer from it. To ignore your mistake, however, is to forego the opportunity you've been given to learn. It is a waste of time to sit on the fence. Go with your gut instincts and trust your intuition. It will connect you with your creator.

Love is the most awesome power in the universe. It can endure such deprivation and neglect without diminishing. Every person must live with the hope that there is someone in the world who will love them. Love them for what they are and not because of what they look like, aspire to, believe in or stand up for. It is our existence that makes us lovable and allows us our place in history.

To see love in someone is like visualising the lights of eternity penetrating you. The aura will buoy your soul and make no obstacle seem insurmountable.

❧

The wave of life must always be treated with respect. It is not wise to take any of creation for granted for it may be wrenched away without warning. Enjoy the exhilaration of catching the wave but be prepared to have to paddle hard to get back out there. Remember that no matter how good the ride it will not last forever and will require continued effort. The waves will keep coming. With each moment of time another opportunity will come your way.

Love is to the earth what air is to our existence.

Our children are the rivulets of our lives, through which run our wisdom but also those thoughts and messages that we'd rather not be giving them. Although they may flood, meander or even dry up at points in time, remember that without them we are no longer complete.

❦

I will care for all that is around me
My needs are not always the most important
I will give of myself and not for myself
I appreciate all that I have
I will help others and spread goodwill
It will then flow back to me like a river.

Guilt is negative and no matter how much you persecute yourself this will not change the past. Guilt is what rises to the surface when we reflect on our lives. It needs to be confronted and put behind you. If this is not done, then all the filter pores may become blocked, which will hinder our appreciation of life. Do not let anyone or anything lay guilt on your doorstep. It is for each of us individually to process how we have dealt with the complexities life has thrown our way.

Confronting death makes us aware of our own mortality, the transience of our existence. Constantly be looking for the next mountain to climb and the next opportunity to be grasped.

There are many things in my life that, if I had the chance, I would do differently the second time around. I know in my heart that I am not ashamed of any specific thing I've done. This simply means that despite my failings I know I have tried my very best. No one can ask for more than that of you.

❧

The lips of a child utter such simple honesty. There is no judgement, prejudice or self-awareness. The beauty is that what the eyes have seen the words express. As adults we need to listen to children to get in touch with our own spirituality. We need their clarity to recognise our emotions and deal with them honestly and positively.

❧

Respect for the beliefs and attitudes of others is a virtue. Human diversity is what makes life an ever changing experience. The earlier in life we realise we cannot change others, the sooner we can develop as caring, loving people.

❧

Love has the power to heal; no matter how deep the wound or how large the scar, love will ease the discomfort.

The search for meaning in life can be elusive. There may be brief moments that seem to have no meaning, which leave us with no tangible reason for continuing. It is essential to ride through these times, as what is awaiting at the other end is a step closer to understanding.

Revenge is the most destructive emotion. Know that retribution against someone who has hurt you will not neutralise the bitterness of your pain. It will eat away at your very being and leave only the bare bones. Be positive and remember that what has already happened cannot be changed.

❦

A mistake is only truly a mistake when we fail to learn from it.

Without some degree of trust we isolate ourselves from humanity. We need it to connect to others and to our enviroment. If uncertain of trusting another person, let it occur in small waves until they merge and blend into a sea. It is not until you take the first step that you begin to grow as a person, and allow the world to restore your confidence.

This world has many more good people in it than it has bad.

❧

The Circle of Life

The strength of the human spirit is immeasurable. By using our minds we have the capacity to conquer any situation. Adapt and be open to change. Your inner spirit will come to the fore if you give it free rein. Muster all determination and fortitude and have faith that strength will come.

～

Anger is dangerous and needs to be expelled as quickly as possible. Take your fury out on a punching bag or a wall or a tree. Let it out when the need arises. Always talk to someone and preferably a person who will not be judgemental. Even taking out the anger on yourself is better than holding it in. Sooner or later it will come to the surface, so why harbour this demon inside you for longer than necessary?

Never assume. Assumption is the mother of all stuff ups.

What do you see when you look in the mirror? Someone proud of their achievements? Someone who has not realised their ambitions, or someone who has been so caught up with routine that they have missed the opportunity? The moment must be seized each and every day.

To love is natural and easy but forgiveness goes against our instincts. Forgiving someone is in many ways the hardest thing to do because it takes strength. It can contort and tear your soul to the point of paralysing it. Summon the courage to forgive those close to you. It will free the spirit within you.

Radiate energy to the world and it will return in vastly greater proportions.

Do not deny yourself the possibility of achieving your enormous potential. Be decisive and ready to conquer. Make or break.

Love is infectious and will always return to those who give it. Smile at people every day and be buoyed by the love you are spreading.

❦

Grief has a nasty habit of shutting off corners of our brain that we cannot revisit. To heal ourselves and resolve trauma in our lives it is essential to acknowledge what has happened in the past. That does not mean *living* in the past, but allowing it the space it needs. In this way we can bear the present and allow ourselves hope and enthusiasm for the future.

Envy and jealousy are destructive. Allowed to run unabated, they will wreak havoc. Appreciate what you *do* have and remember those in a far worse situation than yourself. From this point all aspects of life will take on a new meaning.

There is scope for development and learning every day of our lives. Many of the best lessons will come from simple pleasures. Have the freedom of spirit and clarity of mind to seize these points in time. Surrounded by books and people life gains fullness and an understanding of diversity.

❧

There is so much to be learned by simply talking to people. Every person on this earth has at least one thing they can teach you. Try and gather these snippets of knowledge each day – imagine the results in a couple of years.

❧

Design your life as a garden so the world can marvel
at every branch, stem and petal.

LIFE'S GARDEN

Seductively the aroma engages the attention of all
    within the nose;
Wafts of jasmine intermingle with luscious gardenia;
Each path leads to a new world of discovery;
Rustic tones of red disguise the maple from winter's
    solitude;
Forlorn it will endure nature's bitterness;
With spring comes the hope of prolific growth;
Birds queue to devour the honeysuckle flowers;
Bees swirl in nectar-induced stupor;
Nature is brewing its concoction of delights;
Ready to mesmerise, cajole and coerce the senses into
    submission;
Set to entwine with the souls who have departed our
    midst;
There to display that life marches on;
With or without us it will breathe a new breeze;
Enrage an awesome wave or drench our earth;
With every day there can be no denying;
Their energy, spirit and love will burst forth again.

❧

Music is the elixir of life. It can mimic the heartbeats of our bodies and heal with a magical wand. Allow singing and melody to help you cruise through the difficult parts of living. The resonance it creates in our bodies cannot be replicated with any medicine available.

To be pampered facilitates the healing energy of the universe to flow through you. Any source of touch will soften the jagged bouts of grief or pain. Be surrounded by people who will listen and not judge your reactions, but offer hugs and kisses instead.

Passion is the essence of life, no matter what we are preparing ourselves for. Without it we will flounder like a fish out of water.

❧

Have an unquenchable thirst for knowledge. With every drink you will develop wisdom and power.

Persist in life and life will persist in you.

Gut instinct is a good barometer of our awareness of the world around us. Learn to value what your body tells you and go with it. By doing this we merge with the power of the universe.

❧

Remember that your body is the vehicle of your soul. Ensure your physical being is serviced regularly through diet, exercise and care, or the delivered goods will also be damaged.

Jealousy is a scourge on our society, its power of division and hurt boundless. It may consume with a fervour that is infectious. Focus on what is available rather than what is unobtainable.

Simply let go and your desires will come to you.
Strive for them and they will dissipate at
an alarming rate.

There cannot be enough praise in the world. If there was, people would not suffer from low self-esteem. There is nothing more encouraging when sincere and from the heart.

By saying your work is stressful *you* are
making it stressful!

Society is geared towards consumerism and money. Be aware of the constraints this puts on your lifestyle. Life is not about how far you travel but about what you see and learn while getting to your destination.

Our greatest power comes from being able to serve others. Only once we've been able to do this selflessly are we truly ready to lead others.

Always continue to aspire and dream, for without a dream it cannot become a reality.

Our parents are our link to existence and hence we owe them much. But also remember that our own development will stagnate unless we can break free of them and make independent, guided decisions. Ultimately, as individuals we are accountable only to ourselves.

❧

Patience may be a virtue, but one that is often so difficult to attain. We often want favourable events to happen by rushing them. Relax, have faith in your higher power and the vision will become reality.

❧

Just as it's essential to talk to someone in order to discover what they are like, so you need to look within yourself. Becoming more conscious of your good and bad qualities means being better equipped to improve them. Delve into your soul honestly to see what you are contributing to the world and what you are expecting of it.

We must love ourselves. Once our chalice of love is overflowing we will have a steady stream to pour into others. To be at peace with yourself is to share love with all around you.

❦

Although we would like to believe it, time does *not* heal. Time simply enables acceptance of whatever has happened in our lives. Externally the wound may appear healed, but internally the damage will always be there. Cooperation with the past is the answer to the future. They need to sit harmoniously next to each other.

Absolute acceptance is precious. Surround yourself with people who like you for who you are. You will find that genuine people will attract others like them. The more you care about others the more that love will be returned.

❧

Meditation is a great channel to seeing inside yourself, and one which I use regularly. It will allow you to see reality from the opposite sides of the horizon. The gift afforded by this is that to every problem you will find a solution. Meditating interlaces your energy with the infinite reserves of the universe.

❧

To purify our attitudes to life we must first purge the toxins within our hearts and minds.

Wellbeing is the greatest deterrent to disease.

Strive to resolve problems as soon as they arise. This will ensure the time to deal with new situations with a greater clarity.

❧

I will not procrastinate
I will attack my unenviable tasks head on
Step by step it won't be such a mountain
I will be satisfied for completing my aim
I am proud of my achievements.

❧

The secret to succeeding in life is keeping the lines of communication open. Verbalise, harmonise or apologise, but never put up the shutters.

Hate is a terrible word. The darkness of what it expounds consumes many people. It serves no other purpose than giving those who cannot love somewhere to channel their emotions.

I will not allow negative thoughts into my mind
I will avoid people with negative energy
I want positivity running though my veins
Like my blood, it will then permeate my body
It will sustain and nourish me
It will feed my soul.

Appreciation of life flows from inner harmony. We must be satisfied with the way we look, talk, see, perceive and adapt to our world. Many spend precious time trying to change the things they can't. Having full acceptance of your worth will make you a valuable commodity to everyone.

❧

Happiness doesn't need to be looked for but simply felt and absorbed.

The healing power of touch is infinite. It can penetrate far beyond the physical parameters of our body and lead us back to the right path. Allow touch the chance to resurrect you.

There comes a time in every life when we can no longer blame our past or someone in it for the way we are.

❧

Affirmations are a brilliant way of instilling self-worth. They will strengthen your sense of purpose and give you a springboard from which to attack each day. You must believe in yourself to reach your full potential.

❧

My life is full of love
I feel it through every cell of my body
I appreciate my being and marvel at what I have
The world is abundant in its beauty
I am part of that world.

I will see the light with all its brilliance
It will fill me with security.
I am aware of my faults and accept them fully
My potential will always be great and light will then
radiate out from me.

We have a natural tendency to underestimate the ability of people to deal with an adverse situation, so always try to give more credit than is due.

~

Sincerity can be seen in the eye and felt in the heart.

Writing down feelings and worries in times of uncertainty or difficulty is a wonderful way of learning about yourself. Your perspective on life will radiate further and wider on an infinitely wider plain. Recognising how you were able to deal with a situation will stand you in good stead for the future.

When you walk through the terrain of another's heart you will leave some footprints.

The path to spiritual growth is hard – the hardest.
Embrace it and the rewards are infinite.

As parents and educators we owe it to our children to explain to them about the birds and the bees and, just as importantly, what happens to them when they stop flying.

❧

The Circle of Life

I am a being with infinite love
My iron-clad will always conquers
I am secure in the world
Its energy abounds in me
It nurtures and enriches me
It empowers me to plant the seed of love
In the heart of each person I meet.

❧

Your physical being naturally generates incredible energy when your soul is bearing agony and distress, in order to sustain you. Simply surviving from day to day will make you hopeful that a future exists.

❧

Use the worst thing that has ever been done to you as a reference point of life. From that point of view, most day-to-day things will pale into insignificance and you will find the ability to put even the most stressful situation into context.

❧

Be decisive. The inner relief and freedom that results from making a tough decision will make you feel like a mountain has been lifted off you.

Greed is the vision of men who cannot see what they already have.

Love is very like the planet on which we live. There is day and night, autumn and spring, hot and cold. Love can weather all conditions and reign supreme if allowed to.

In a world full of expectations our lives need balance. A comparison between what we want and what we really need. Don't let the game of life pass you by because you want to win at the end. Try to lead after each quarter and the final result will never be in question.

❧

The universe will unravel its storyline as it intends to. Our part is to accept the role given and to perform it with pride and passion. Each scene is necessary to get us to the current stage of the performance.

❧

Although we would love to change the world and the constant injustice in it, there are many things we just can't change. But we can choose to make a difference by helping others wherever we can, and hopefully changing the world a little.

❧

Search for the ultimate and only purpose. A source of growth and enrichment. The very essence of motivation, enthusiasm and life itself. Be true to your instincts and heart; only then will you be able to find love and the universal power it will bestow on you.

Walter Mikac
To Have and To Hold

On 28 April 1996, Walter Mikac lost his wife, Nanette, and two daughters, six-year-old Alannah and three-year-old Madeline. They were shot dead, along with 32 other innocent people, during the Port Arthur massacre in Tasmania.

To Have and To Hold is Walter's tribute to Nanette and the girls, and their uniqueness. Walter recounts their early life together, their love for each other and the years of happiness they shared – all of which have sustained him through grief.

He tackles with courage and honesty aspects of bereavement that are rarely acknowledged. He has also found himself thrust into the media spotlight, his grief exposed for the world to see.

Walter Mikac is an ordinary person who, through no fault of his own, has been put in an extraordinary position. Coping with the unimaginable loss of his family has led Walter down a spiritual path of discovery – one of hope and belief that the circle of life continues. His grace and dignity in the face of tragedy have inspired a nation.

'You come away from *To Have and to Hold* with a renewed faith in the human spirit . . . nobody could remain untouched by this book.'
THE AGE